All in
Family

Contents

Features

WORD BUILDER

Turn to page 5 and discover an easy way to remember complicated things.

PROFILE

Read **On the Snail Trail** on page 6 and learn how one person's hobby has led to the discovery of many new species.

TRY THIS!

What happens to leftover food? Turn to **Make a Mould Terrarium** on page 11 to conduct your own experiment.

IN FOCUS

Would you like to live and work among wild animals? Read an e-mail from a wildlife worker in **Animal Refuge** on page 24.

SITESEEING • PLANTS & ANIMALS •

What do you call a group of elephants?

Visit www.infosteps.co.uk
for more about THE ANIMAL KINGDOM.

Living Things

In the past many people thought all living things were either plants or animals. We now know that many other types of living things exist. While many living things have some similarities, each type is different in some way. Dogs and cats have four legs, a tail and eat meat, but we only have to look at them to know they are not the same.

To help people understand these similarities and differences scientists have developed a way of classifying all living things. They start with one of the five largest groupings, such as animals, and continue to divide the group until they reach a specific animal such as the lion. The science of arranging living things in this way is called taxonomy.

Carl Linnaeus (1707–1778)

Carl Linnaeus is known as the father of modern plant and animal classification. He travelled on many expeditions, discovering a huge variety of new plants.

Linnaeus thought plants and animals were being classified poorly so he carefully gathered information on 7,700 species of plants and 4,400 species of animals. His work was so accurate and detailed that his classification system is still used today.

WORD BUILDER

It can be useful to make up simple sentences to help us remember complicated things. These are called *mnemonics.* A mnemonic for remembering the classification system of living things is:

King Philip Comes Over For Good Spaghetti.

For more about classification turn to **Getting Specific** on page 16.

The Five Kingdoms

There are several million different kinds of living things on our planet. From the smallest dust mite to the mighty whale and from the tiniest fern to the tallest tree, each living thing can be classified into one of five kingdoms. Each kingdom includes living things that are similar in some ways, but they also have features that differ from one another. All living things, no matter how different and in which kingdom, are made of cells.

The largest kingdom is the animal kingdom. More than a million animal species have been discovered. However, scientists believe there are at least another eight million species in the animal kingdom still to be discovered.

On the Snail Trail

As a hobby some people collect stamps, while others collect rocks or plants. Pete Cresswell (born 1938) collects snail shells. He began collecting the shells when he was 12 years old. He now has more than 120,000 shells in his collection which includes some as small as a pinhead and others as large as a tennis ball. Over the years he has found many new species of snails. Pete has even had two species of snails named after him.

Monera Kingdom: small single-celled living things called bacteria

Protista Kingdom: large usually single-celled living things including **amoeba**

Scientists classify living things by their structure, whether they are mobile and what they eat.

Fungi Kingdom: multi-celled living things, including mushrooms, that absorb food

Animal Kingdom: multi-celled living things that take in, or ingest, food for digestion

Plant Kingdom: multi-celled living things that **photosynthesize** food

The Monera Kingdom

All around us are millions of micro-organisms that are too small to be seen without a microscope. These micro-organisms are classified into two kingdoms, monera and protista. In the kingdom of monera there is one broad kind of living thing, bacteria.

Bacteria, which have only one cell, are the oldest and simplest creatures on Earth. They grow by cell division. When a cell divides it produces two identical cells. If conditions are right these cells then divide, as do the resulting cells and so on. However, ideal conditions rarely exist. If they did, the entire planet would quickly be overrun by bacteria.

Bacteria can only be seen under a microscope.

The Protista Kingdom

The kingdom of protista is the strangest of all. It seems to contain life forms that don't fit into any other kingdom. One of the most common members, the amoeba, can be found in rivers and ponds and on the surfaces of leaves and water plants. Under a microscope amoeba look like grey blobs that change shape as they move along.

Like bacteria amoeba reproduce by cell division. Some amoeba can cause serious illness while others eat bacteria that could be harmful to humans.

Under a microscope it is possible to see the false foot of an amoeba, which appears to push the amoeba along. This isn't a real foot. It's only a bulge in the cell wall.

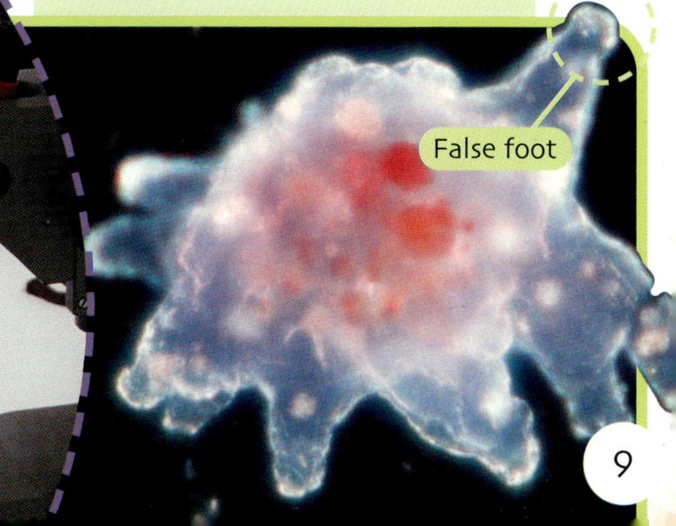

The Fungi Kingdom

Although mushrooms may look similar to some plants, they are not classified as plants. Mushrooms actually belong to the fungi kingdom. Because fungi are not able to photosynthesize they are not classified as plants. Fungi, which include mushrooms, yeasts and mildew, are found in an amazing variety of shapes and sizes. Some fungi absorb nutrients directly from soil, some absorb rotting matter and some absorb nutrients from other living things.

Fungi can be a problem for humans. Athlete's foot is a fungus that absorbs human skin! Other fungi are beneficial. Penicillin, a type of fungi **mould**, is one of the most important **antibiotics** ever discovered.

Fungi don't contain **chlorophyll** and can't make their own food. Instead they absorb food from their surroundings.

TRY THIS!

Make a Mould Terrarium

Find out what happens to leftover food!

You will need:

- 1 disposable clear glass or plastic container with a lid
- adhesive tape
- water
- 4 or 5 small pieces of different foods such as bread, fruit, vegetables, cheese, biscuits or cake

Method:

1. Dip each piece of food into water. Place the pieces in the container so they are close to each other, but not all in a heap.
2. Put on the lid of the container and tape around the edge to seal it. Put the container somewhere safe so it won't be knocked over.
3. Look at the terrarium every day. For the first few days you probably won't see much. Soon, however, you should see some mould growing.

Observations:

- Which food started getting mouldy first?
- What colour is the mould? How many different colours do you see?
- Do different kinds of mould grow on different types of food?
- Does everything in your terrarium become mouldy?

IMPORTANT

Don't use meat or fish because these would smell very bad after a few days. Throw out your terrarium after about two weeks. Don't reuse the container or even open the lid. Mould is dangerous for some people to smell or breathe.

The Plant Kingdom

All plants make their own food from air, sunlight and water in a process called photosynthesis. They use a substance called chlorophyll to capture light energy. This results in their green colour.

All plants except mosses contain special tissues that carry water, minerals and other nutrients throughout the plant. The **xylem** tissue carries water and nutrients from the roots to the leaves. The **phloem** tissue carries food made by photosynthesis in the leaves to the other parts of the plant.

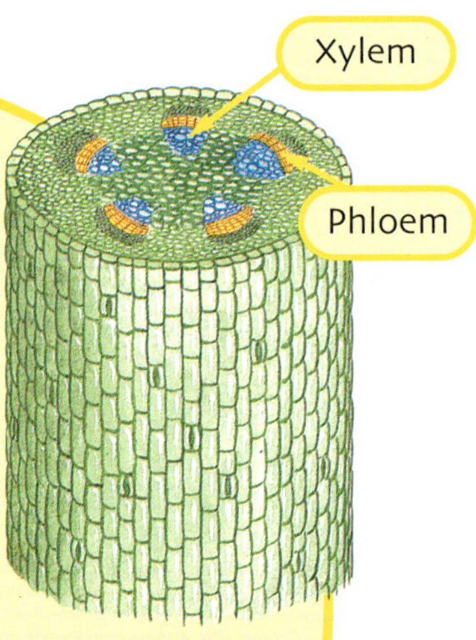

Cells in the stem of a plant contain xylem and phloem which transport water, minerals and nutrients throughout the plant.

Common Plant Phyla

Mosses
- have no system of veins
- never have flowers
- grow on the ground, rocks and other plants
- reproduce by **spores**

Ferns
- have a system of veins
- never have flowers
- grow on the ground and other plants
- reproduce by spores
- provide shade for other plants

Conifers
- have a system of veins
- never have flowers
- grow on the ground
- reproduce by seeds within cones
- provide protection from erosion

Monocots
- have a system of veins
- always have flowers
- seeds sprout one first leaf
- are not woody
- include grains, dates, bananas

Dicots
- have a system of veins
- always have flowers
- seeds sprout two first leaves
- are woody
- include most trees, vines, fruits, vegetables

The Animal Kingdom

Humans are classified in the largest kingdom of living things, the animal kingdom. Animals are different from other living things in many ways. Unlike the members of the monera and protista kingdoms, animals are made up of many cells which are organized into tissues that perform special tasks. Animals can also move around, unlike plants and fungi.

There are at least 33 different phyla in the animal kingdom. Many animals are so small they can only be seen with a microscope. Creatures without backbones, called invertebrates, make up the largest group of known animals. Creatures with backbones, called vertebrates, make up the rest.

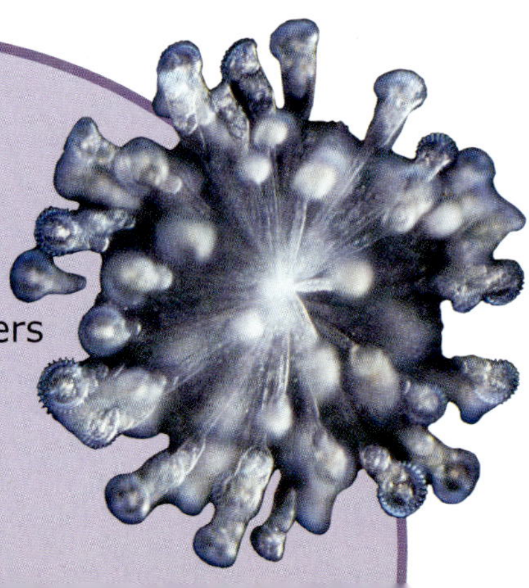

Rotifers are microscopic animals that live in fresh water. The largest rotifers are about 0.5 millimetres long.

Common Animal Phyla

Chordata
- vertebrates
- includes fish, mammals, birds, reptiles, amphibians
- 45,000 known species

Arthropoda
- invertebrates with external skeletons, jointed bodies and legs
- includes insects, spiders, crabs
- 500,000 known species

Mollusca
- invertebrates with soft bodies usually enclosed in hard shells
- includes slugs, snails, squids, octopuses
- 100,000 known species

Echinodermata
- invertebrates
- have spiny skin and no clear front or back
- includes sea stars, sea urchins
- 6,000 known species

Cnidaria
- invertebrates
- have tentacles that sting
- includes jellyfish, coral
- 9,500 known species

Getting Specific

Linnaeus' system of classification is like a giant filing system. Scientists sort organisms into groups based on special features they have in common. Follow this example to find the brown bear and its closest relatives.

Kingdom

Here is a group of animals. All animals are many-celled and get energy from the food they eat.

Phylum

From the animals shown above, those that share a major characteristic, in this case vertebrates, are selected.

Class

From the phylum of vertebrates, the class that shares the characteristic of being mammals is selected.

Order

From the mammals, the order of **Carnivora** is selected. Most members of this group are **carnivores** and eat meat, though some such as the Giant Panda are **herbivores**.

Family

Members of the bear family have heavy bodies, a large skull, thick legs and a short tail. Unlike most carnivores they rely heavily on vegetation for their food.

Genus

The Asiatic black bear and the brown bear belong to the same genus.

Species

Although the Asiatic black bear and the brown bear share many characteristics they do not interbreed so they are two species.

A Cat's Tale

Dividing living things into kingdoms and then the kingdoms into phyla helps us to group creatures into broad categories. It is quite simple to understand the differences between plants and animals or people and sea stars. It is not quite as easy, however, to state the similarities and differences between all cats.

Do you know that there are 36 different species of wild cats? More than three-quarters of the world's wild cats are small cats. You are probably familiar with big cats such as the tiger, jaguar and leopard, but have you heard of the serval, caracal or Scottish wild cat? These are all small cats.

One main difference between the small cats, genus *Felis*, and the big cats, genus *Panthera*, is that small cats can purr when breathing in and out but not roar, while large cats can roar but purr only when breathing out. The cheetah, however, can do both so it is a separate genus, *Acinonyx*.

Small Cats

Small cats are very similar in appearance and behaviour to big cats. While big cats will hunt prey larger than themselves small cats usually hunt for rats and birds.

Serval, *Felis serval*

Caracal, *Felis caracal*

Scottish wild cat, *Felis sylvestris*

Small wild cats are possibly the ancestors of the domestic cat. Some have similar markings to a tabby.

One Species, One Hundred Faces

There are many different breeds of the domestic dog species. No other species of animal has such a range of shapes, sizes, colours, coats and personalities. However, all domestic dogs share certain characteristics that go back to their common origin, the wolf.

Dogs belong to the family called Canidae and are often referred to as canids. As early canids began to hang around people's dwellings looking for food, they became tamer. Because they had no need to hunt for food, their jaws, bodies and brains became smaller than those of the wolf.

Over the centuries people began to crossbreed animals with desirable traits such as size, an ability to retrieve or hunt, a long coat or a short coat. Gradually, a wide variety of dog types developed. Dogs have **evolved** in the company of people and depend on them for survival. A dog is often called "a man's best friend".

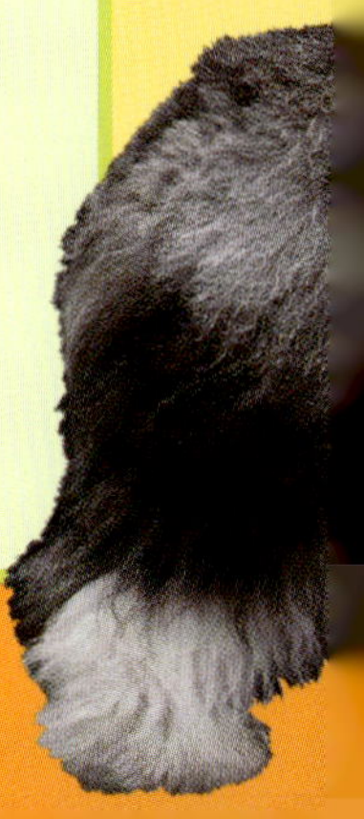

About 12,000 years ago in what is now Israel hunters and gatherers placed a body in a grave with its hand cradling a puppy. This is the earliest fossil evidence of domestic dogs.

The howling chorus of a pack of wolves can be heard for about ten kilometres. Domestic dogs have been tamed to be obedient, but they too can be noisy.

Living Together

Loners are not common in the animal kingdom. Most species of animals live in pairs or in larger social groups. Living together provides company and protection for the members of the group. Many birds flock, feed and nest together. Herds of mammals graze together and fish swim together in groups called schools.

When different species live together in a close relationship it is called symbiosis. There are three forms of symbiosis: commensalism, mutualism and parasitism. Commensalism occurs if one species benefits while the other is unaffected. In mutualism both organisms benefit. In parasitism one organism is harmful to another.

Tapeworms feed on food in the intestines of people and other animals. In this instance one organism benefits while another is harmed. This type of symbiosis is called parasitism.

Epiphytes are plants which grow above the ground's surface using other plants for support. By growing on other plants the epiphytes can reach positions where the light is better.

Tropical orchids, like many rainforest plants, are epiphytes. They absorb nutrients from the host tree and have dangling aerial roots to absorb water from the damp air.

Elephants are very social animals and live in family groups which sometimes join larger groups of elephants. The family is led by an old experienced female.

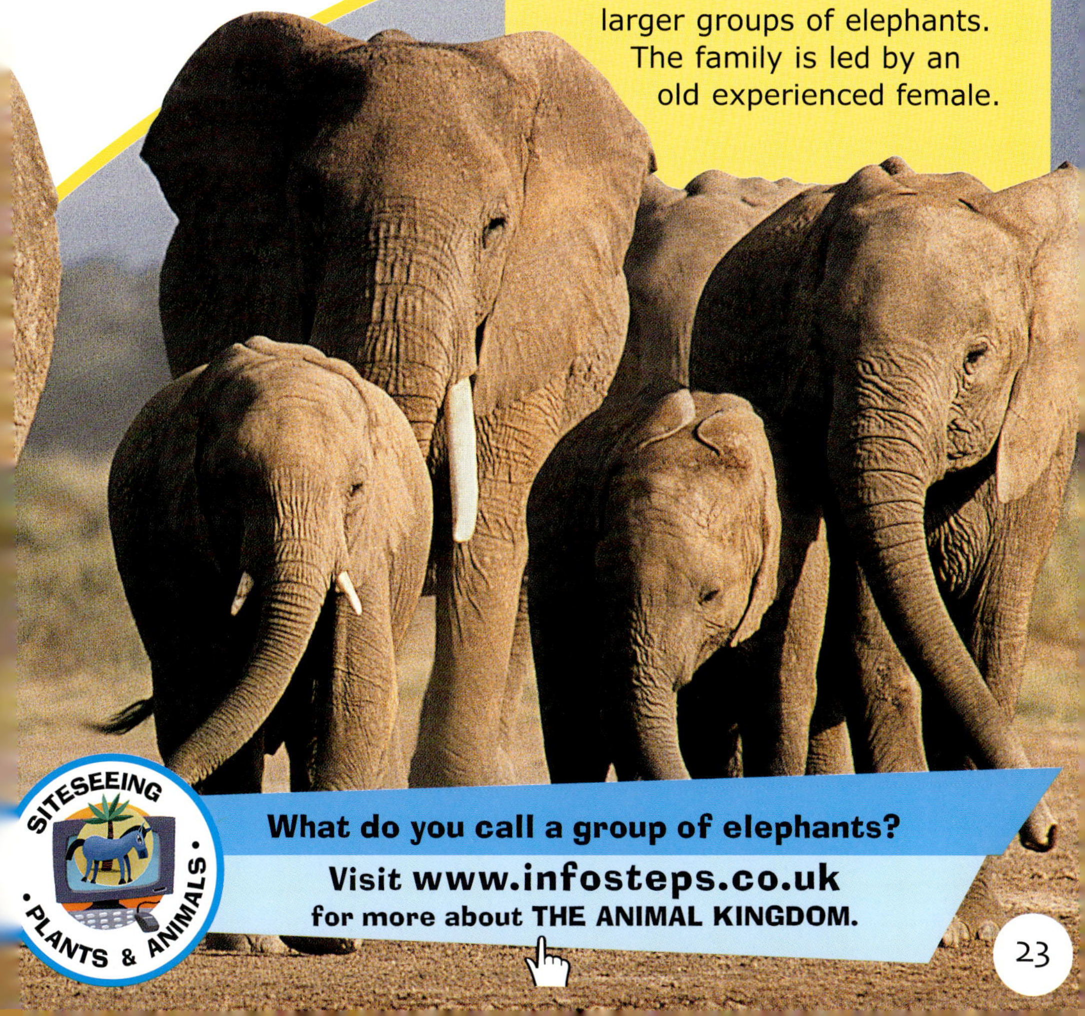

SITESEEING PLANTS & ANIMALS

What do you call a group of elephants?

Visit www.infosteps.co.uk
for more about THE ANIMAL KINGDOM.

Animal Refuge

Marlice Jansen van Vuuren is a wildlife worker. She works on a farm in Namibia, Africa that is an orphanage for neglected or injured wild animals.

Dear Marlice,

My name is Chelsea and I'm 11 years old. I saw some photographs of you working with animals at a wildlife rehabilitation farm in Africa. I have loved animals all my life. I have a dog named Ziggy and two rabbits. I am very curious about your job and would like to ask you some questions:

• The baby baboon in the photo is adorable! Does it have a name? Is it an orphan?

• How long have you been working with animals?

• What's the hardest part of your job?

Please write back.

Yours sincerely,
Chelsea

Dear Chelsea,

The baby baboon's name is Violet, and yes, she is an orphan. I love many animals, but baboons are my favourite animal.

My parents have looked after sick and orphaned wild animals on our farm since I was a baby, so I have always been surrounded by animals. I am now a tour guide for guests who visit the farm.

I love my job. The hardest parts for me are returning the animals to the wild and not always being able to heal a sick animal.

Lots of animal hugs,
Marlice

PS I've attached a photo of me with two baboons. The big one is Violet—she has grown a lot! The baby is Leonie.

Nature's Cycles

In any **biome** the organisms in the five kingdoms depend on one another for their survival. Living things also rely on non-living elements such as the sun, soil, air and water.

A community of living and non-living things is called an ecosystem. Water, oxygen and other elements vital for life are recycled through the ecosystem again and again. These cycles in nature are fairly stable, but human activities that change the environment can disturb them. It is important that people protect the delicate balance of Earth's environment.

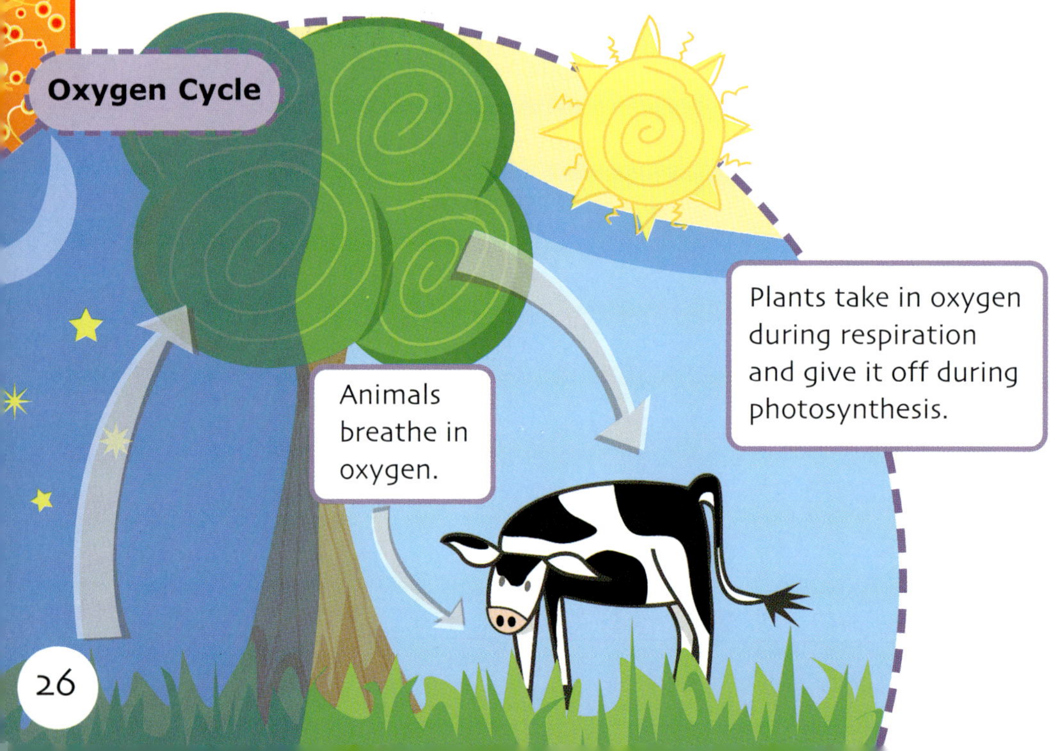

Cycles in Nature

The water cycle is just one of many cycles in nature. The oxygen and carbon cycles are also important cycles. Living things take in water, carbon, nitrogen and oxygen and they use them to live and grow. If these resources were used only once they would run out. All animals and plants respire, or breathe, grow and eventually die and decompose.

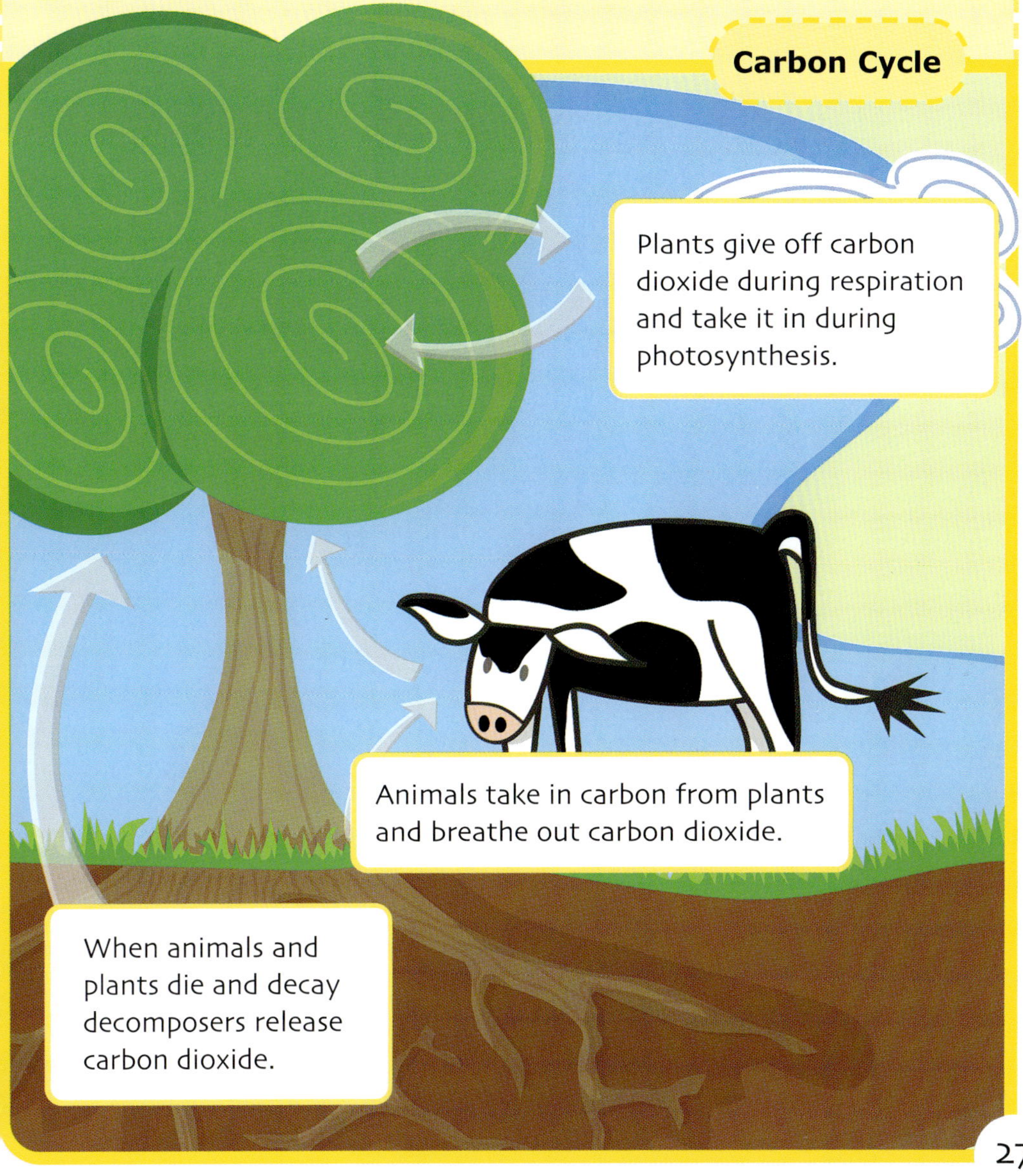

Where We Belong

The main difference between human beings and other living things is the human brain. People have used their intelligence to develop language, technology and culture. They can adapt their environment to live almost anywhere on Earth.

Many features of the human body have characteristics in common with other living things. In particular humans share some characteristics with the order of mammals known as primates. There are more than 300 species of primates including apes, monkeys, aye-ayes, lemurs and human beings.

Primates have hands with five fingers and feet with five toes. Many primate species have thumbs and big toes capable of grasping. Most primates also have good eyesight and can judge depth.

Howler monkeys like many species of monkeys are highly intelligent primates. They grasp food and branches with their hands and feet and they use twigs as tools.

As groups or nations, people develop cultures and traditions that include art, music, literature and sports.

Glossary

amoeba – a very small form of living organism with only one cell. An amoeba moves by changing its body shape. A false foot drags the rest of the amoeba in its direction.

antibiotic – a substance that is able to stop the growth of harmful bacteria

biome – a large area with a particular community of plants and animals and with a particular climate

Carnivora – an order of mammals that have powerful jaws and specialized teeth suited for tearing and eating meat

carnivore – an animal that eats meat

chlorophyll – the green colouring in plants. Light makes chlorophyll change carbon dioxide and water into food.

evolve – to change slowly, sometimes over millions of years

herbivore – an animal that eats mainly plants

mould – a furry fungus that grows on old food or a damp surface

phloem – tissue in a plant that transports sugar, mineral salts and other nutrients

photosynthesis – the process in which a plant uses light to change carbon dioxide and water into food

spore – a cell that can grow into an organism

xylem – tissue in a plant that transports water and mineral salts from the roots to the leaves

Index

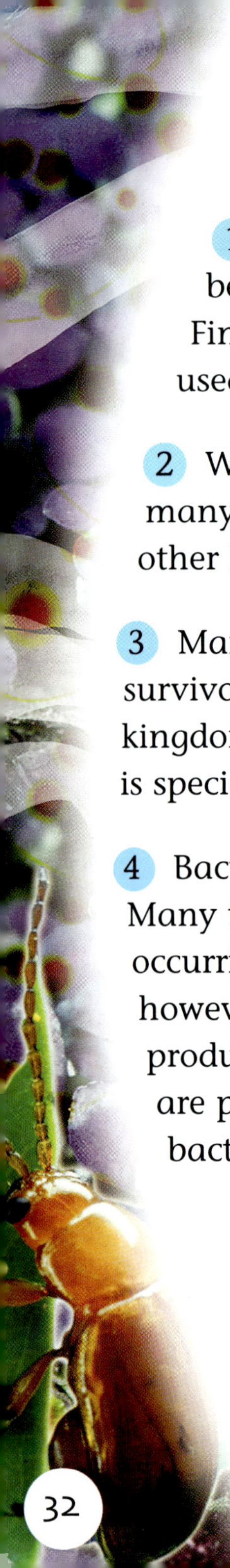

Research Starters

1 Scientists believe we have only discovered between 10% and 20% of all living creatures. Find out how technology is being developed and used to discover new forms of life.

2 We get our energy from the food we eat, but many creatures use different methods. Find out how other life forms keep themselves fuelled.

3 Many scientists believe that the most likely survivors of a major catastrophe from the animal kingdom would be insects. Research to discover what is special about these creatures.

4 Bacteria are often thought of as being dangerous. Many types of food poisoning are caused by bacteria occurring in undercooked or infected meat. Bacteria, however, also play an important part in food production. Research to find out some foods that are produced by using bacteria. What are these bacteria called?